In h... aan Wedeland,

Sander Griffioen

UNBELIEF AND REVOLUTION

LECTURE XI

GUILLAUME GROEN VAN PRINSTERER

THE HISTORY OF THE REVOLUTION IN ITS FIRST PHASE: THE PREPARATION (TILL 1789)

lecture eleven from

UNBELIEF AND REVOLUTION

A SERIES OF LECTURES IN HISTORY

edited and translated by
Harry Van Dyke

in collaboration with
Donald Morton

THE GROEN VAN PRINSTERER FUND   1973   AMSTERDAM

Published by THE GROEN VAN PRINSTERER FUND, c/o Hoofd-gebouw 13A-31, Free University, Amsterdam.

PRINTED IN THE NETHERLANDS by Vis-Druk, Alphen aan den Rijn.

Cover: Guillaume Groen van Prinsterer. Detail from a lithograph by N.J.W. de Roode. With permission from the *Rijksprenten Kabinet, Rijksmuseum*, Amsterdam.

FOREWORD

Guillaume Groen van Prinsterer (1801-1876), the important Dutch historian and statesman, was educated in law and the classics at Leiden.

As secretary to the King he was a close observer of the Belgian Revolt of 1830, which raised weighty constitutional and historical questions. About this time he was led to a whole-hearted evangelical faith through the Christian ministry of J.H. Merle d'Aubigné, who also introduced him to the works of Edmund Burke. Reading these strengthened Groen's growing anti-revolutionary political convictions.

Later Groen entered Parliament, where he became the greatest nineteenth-century opponent of the dominant liberal movement and its eminent spokesman, Johan Thorbecke. The Thorbecke–Groen van Prinsterer debates constitute a distinguished and crucial chapter in the parliamentary history of the Netherlands. Groen championed constitutional monarchy and parliamentary rights and resisted the totalitarian tendencies of liberal democracy. Although he was increasingly isolated, Groen's systematic dissent and consistent evangelical testimony resulted in the strengthening of parliamentary government and the growth of liberty.

Meanwhile Groen served for many decades as archivist to the royal family, acquiring just fame throughout Europe as editor of the multi-volume *Archives de la Maison d'Orange-Nassau*. He was the pioneer of scientific historiography in the

Netherlands, and was in professional contact with such leading historians as Guizot, Gachard and Ranke.

Groen was the leader of the struggle for educational freedom in his country, where today parochial and private Christian schools stand on an equal footing with secular ones. For this, and for his efforts to keep modernism from dominating in pulpit and seminary, he was widely known. It is not surprising, then, that he received an extraordinary welcome as a speaker at the fifth international conference of the Evangelical Alliance, held in Amsterdam in 1867. Groen van Prinsterer brought the evangelical party in the Netherlands back to involvement in public life. He is the link between the evangelical revival of the 1820's and the spiritual awakening of the 1880's, between Bilderdijk and Da Costa the poets, and Abraham Kuyper the emancipator.

The book *Ongeloof en Revolutie*, published in the summer of 1847, is a classic statement of Christian anti-revolutionary thought. Its central thesis is that the French revolution of 1789 was prepared by the Revolution in European thought during the preceding century, a Revolution which the author contends was the fruit of Unbelief. The new political philosophy, Groen argues, which recognized no authority beyond man and his reason, was a natural consequence of that wholesale skepticism by which the Enlightenment revolted against God and His ordinances for human life. In this book Groen pictures the Revolution as at last breaking visibly to the surface in 1789, with all the enthusiasm, determination and rigour of an apostate religious movement having its day. Any interpretation of the French revolution and its aftermath which fails to fathom the religious character of the events is considered fundamentally unsound.

It is noteworthy that Groen's appraisal antedates by

fully a decade De Tocqueville's study on the *Ancien Régime et
la Révolution*, in which he wrote that the course of the French
revolution was preponderantly influenced by the eighteenth
century's total rejection of the old religion. But where De
Tocqueville added, "without another's being put in its place,"
Groen commented: "the other religion was that of Rousseau! " [1] Had he known Groen's book, Carl Becker probably
would not have written what he did as late as 1932: "Not until
our own time have historians been sufficiently detached from
religions to understand that the Revolution, in its later stages
especially, took on the character of a religious crusade."[2]

Owing to its deep religious roots, Groen explained, the
Revolution had not ended with the Restoration but had
merely entered upon another phase. As long as men refused to
break with its spirit the Revolution would continue to gnaw at
the foundations of society, and would even render inevitable
such flare-ups as that of 1830. The perception of its
permanence is thus inherent in Groen's vision of the Revolution. It is from this perception that *Unbelief and Revolution*
derives its prophetic tone.[3] The author was not surprised by
the explosive events of 1848, the year following the publication of his lectures, for he believed that the only effective
antidote against the Revolution is the Gospel. *Unbelief and*

---

[1] "die andere rel. was die van Rousseau! " This is the actual
reading of a gloss in Groen's handwriting found on p. 229 of his copy
of *L'Ancien Régime et la Révolution*, now in the Koninklijke Biblio-
theek in The Hague. De Tocqueville's epoch-making book was published in 1856, while Groen's lectures were held in 1845-46.

[2] Carl L. Becker, *The Heavenly City of the Eighteenth-Century
Philosophers* (Yale Paperbound ed., 1959), p. 155.

[3] In a political tract of 1860 Groen explicitly diagnosed his time
as one of "permanent revolution." See *Le Parti anti-révolutionnaire et*

Revolution denies that the secularization of public affairs is beneficial, and challenges Christians not to "stay away" from politics.

Groen predicted the drift of Western politics to the left. He pointed to the ideological consistency of communist socialism and anticipated its triumphs. He regarded radicalism and moderate liberalism as two branches on the same tree, sharing a common root; and he warned against the weakness of a conservative opposition based solely on cautious self-interest. Groen could find no meaningful choices within the existing political spectrum, where, on his view, the left were radical believers, the centre were moderate or resigned believers, and the right were disbelievers, who, for failing to understand the causes of the drift, could only react against its nastier effects. To choose from among these alternatives was for him only to choose the speed at which the principles of the Revolution would be applied. Groen spent his life attempting to chart a new course for politics, along *anti*-revolutionary Christian-historical lines.

No work by Groen van Prinsterer has ever before been published in English. The reader may find it useful, however, to consult the article by G. H. Hospers, Sr., "Groen van Prinsterer and His Book," in the *Evangelical Quarterly*, volume VII (1935), pages 267-286.

From its inception in 1955 the translation of *Ongeloof en Revolutie* has been a communal project under the general supervision of Professor H. Evan Runner. Work on it was first begun by members of the Groen van Prinsterer Society, a

---

confessionnel dans l'Eglise Réformée des Pays-Bas (Amsterdam, 1860), p. 31: "la Révolution en permanence."

student club in Grand Rapids, Michigan. Later, the major portion of a first draft was completed by Professor Henry Van Zyl. In 1963 the entire manuscript was passed on to the present editor.

The translation, of which this is the first instalment, is based upon the first edition of 1847 in order to retain the helpful summaries, the more explicit connective phrases and transitional paragraphs, and the warm, personal references to the original lecture setting—all of which the author deleted when he revised his book in 1868. From the revised edition, however, we retain the additional footnotes (marked by a †) and those stylistic improvements that helped avoid needless repetition. Significant variations in the text are also indicated. Insofar as practicable, the citation references and other bibliographical data are adapted to modern usage.

The present publication, made possible by a grant from the Groen van Prinsterer Fund, is intended as the first in a series which, the Lord willing, will see into print the whole of *Unbelief and Revolution*. The following pages contain one of the key chapters of the book, together with the author's prefaces, which serve to introduce it. Cross references to chapters not yet available are included in provisional form (e.g. "se above, p. 00"). The Bibliography and Chronology, drawn up by the editor, pertain only to the present chapter.

The first draft of *Lecture XI* was prepared by Aaldert Mennega more than fifteen years ago. We gratefully acknowledge the late Professor H. Smitskamp's kind permission to use any of the explanatory notes from his modern Dutch edition of 1951.

Amsterdam, *September 1973*

THE EDITOR

ONGELOOF EN REVOLUTIE.

EENE REEKS VAN HISTORISCHE

VOORLEZINGEN,

DOOR

Mʳ. G. GROEN VAN PRINSTERER.

LEIDEN,
S. EN J. LUCHTMANS.
1847.

UNBELIEF AND REVOLUTION

TABLE OF CONTENTS

PREFACES

PREFACE
[extract]

The following lectures constitute an essay in demonstrating from history that there is a natural and necessary relation between *unbelief* and *revolution*; that the school of thought which, as a result of the self-exaltation of man, holds sway today in Constitutional Law and in learning—although not uncontested—arose from a rejection of the Gospel.

I have attempted to make clear from the evidence of past experience that this pernicious school systematically overturned the foundations of truth and law in order to erect airy castles; that its progress, which is commonly praised to the skies, leads men along the path of legitimate deduction towards full-blown atheism and radicalism; that its principle, once endorsed, leaves its advocates no defence against consistent application save the forcible arrest of an altogether logical development.

From the deadliness of the fruit I have drawn the conclusion—without forcing the argument, I believe—that the tree on which this fruit grows is no tree of life. The aim should be, not to nurse the poisonous plant, but to root it out. I have come to the conclusion, in other words, that in the field of politics, too, a man cannot reap but what he has sown: just as a difference in soil cannot change the peculiar character of the seed, so likewise the alteration of circumstances will not produce any changes in the revolutionary crop. Quite to the contrary, the inevitability of the failure stems from the very nature of the experiment. As the denial of the living God is related to disorder, injustice and slavery, so the union of freedom with law and order, like the philosophers' stone, is sought in vain outside submission to the highest Lawgiver and King.

But enough already! I could easily state too boldly in advance what is but carefully and gradually brought out in the book itself. I could easily insure, by introducing the contents too abruptly, that the book would be adjudged unfit for use and too objectionable to be read; that the work in which I have for the first time recorded at some length the whole of my Christian-historical view would scornfully or indignantly be laid aside.

Except for a few minor changes, I am releasing the text as it was delivered orally during the winter of 1845-46 in the library at my home before a small number of friends whose interest in the case and whose goodwill for the speaker were assured. Initially I had not intended a speedy publication. I had planned instead to revise these essays carefully, the result of extended research and mature deliberation though they already were; and, mindful of the adage, *Nonum prematur in annum* ['Wait eight years'], to bring them to greater completeness through continued investigation and reflection. Soon, however, I became convinced that neither the subject of this study nor the crisis of our age made such plans advisable or such postponement permissible. When one ventures to deal with weighty questions, anything tending towards completeness belongs to the realm of unfulfillable wishes. Here in our country, too, a battle is being waged about History and Constitutional Law. It is a contest from which I do not wish to remain aloof. This struggle touches upon the most cherished and sacred interests of our fatherland and of mankind, and directly or indirectly concerns either the recognition or the neglect of the Light of the world and hence the salvation of immortal souls. Therefore, in view of the weight of the matter and the urgency of the moment, I was not allowed to forget, out of selfish scruples about publicity, that the hour of peril is not the hour of preparation; that when the enemy's sword glitters on all sides one ought not to sharpen and polish his weapons but rather to put them to use.

. . . .

I conclude with the declaration that, over against all the wisdom of men and in awareness of my own frailty, I have for a slogan two words as the earnest of victory: *It is written!* and *It has come to pass!* —a foundation that will stand against any artillery, a root that will hold against every whirlwind of philosophic unbelief. *It has come to pass!* This is History, which is also the flaming script of the holy God. *It is written!* This is Holy Scripture, which, since event and doctrine are inseparable, is also the historical Scripture. History! as it is formed, not just by the succession of deeds, but especially by the unfolding of ideas. History! as it receives its beginning and meaning and direction and unity from the facts of Revelation. Holy Scripture! as it dictates its own law to the students of Scripture, in the foolishness of the Cross confounding the profundity of philosopher or sophist with the humble faith of little children. Holy Scripture! as it bears witness to the Lamb that was slain, to the rod out of the stem of Jesse and the unconquerable Lion from the tribe of Judah, David's son and David's Lord, God and man, Mediator or Judge, who, after holding out the staff of grace in vain, has in His hand a rod of iron to smite a stiffnecked people. History and Scripture! as they in unison, under the forfeited blessing of a measure of longsuffering that exceeds all expectations, direct the penitent sinner to Him who has revealed Himself in all the glory of His perfections also on Dutch soil; Whose promise and threat, *Those that honour Me will I honour, but those that despise Me shall be lightly esteemed*, has been fulfilled in the expanse of blessing by which a nation that was hardly a nation was elevated to a first rank among the Powers, and in the expanse of humiliation and misery which the denial of His holy Name has brought upon an ungrateful posterity . . . .

August 1847

PREFACE TO THE SECOND EDITION

For this second edition, just a few words by way of introduction.

Scarcely had *Unbelief and Revolution* made its public appearance, when the Revolution of 1848 broke loose over France and Europe.

The text is virtually unchanged. In the notes, however, by adding references to my subsequent writings, I have endeavoured to turn to profit the experience of twenty years in an exceptionally revolutionary era.

Consequently it will become evident that my conviction, as it has crystallized into a Christian-historical or anti-revolutionary world outlook, has not just remained the same, but has grown stronger: for all its merits, modern society, having fallen into bondage to the theory of unbelief, is increasingly being led on to a *systematic denial of the living God*.

July 1868   Gr. v. Pr.

LECTURE XI

THE HISTORY OF THE REVOLUTION IN ITS FIRST PHASE: THE PREPARATION (TILL 1789)

FOR THE BENEFIT OF THOSE WHO ARE with us for the first time tonight, let me begin with a few words about the standpoint, the aim and the development of these lectures.

Our standpoint is that of the Christian who desires to glory in nothing but Christ and Him crucified. In religion, morality and justice, in the home or in the state, the Christian acknowledges no wisdom or truth that does not begin with submission of heart and mind to Revelation. He not only traces and notes the guidance of Providence in history, as does the deist; but, faithful and dedicated to the Gospel, he acknowledges and awaits the solution to the enigmas of the history of mankind in the first coming and triumphant return of the Saviour. He loves the appearing of the Redeemer because he discerns in it, in the words of the historian Von Müller, "the fulfilment of all hopes, the culmination of all philosophy, the explanation of all revolutions, the key to all the seeming contradictions of the physical and moral world, and life and immortality."[1]

As for our aim: to each one of us comes the word, "As every man hath received the gift, even so minister the same one to another, as good stewards of the manifold grace of God."[2] After all the labour I have spent in studying history, I consider it my calling to witness on this terrain to the truth that is in Christ. This I wish to do also in these gatherings. I propose to demonstrate, in broad outline, that the history of the past sixty years, with its outpourings of wickedness, has been the fruit and manifestation of systematic unbelief.

The development of the lectures has been as follows. We began by examining the former positive constitutional law and came to the conclusion that the Revolution cannot be explained simply from a reaction against certain principles, forms of government, or abuses. Next we found that the perversion of constitutional law was not by itself the source of the Revolution. Thus we cleared our path toward discovering the real cause. We found it in the apostasy from the Gospel. We saw how religious decline had already begun to threaten dissolution of the states when the blessing of the Reformation stemmed the tide. We saw also, however, how the truth, which was set on a candlestick in the sixteenth century, was once again, through apathy and moral degeneracy, put under a bushel as the seventeenth century wore

---

[1] Johann von Müller, quoted in my *Proeve*, pp. 47-76.

[2] I Peter 4:10.

on. As a result, the philosophy of the eighteenth century, that dark night of unbelief, succeeded in passing off its will-o'-the-wisp for light of the sun.

In the last three lectures I have tried to show that unbelief, as the germ of error and corruption, must in theory and practice culminate in atheism and radicalism, two realities which are usually but incorrectly held to be mere excesses of the unbelieving doctrine of liberty.

Now I shall turn to history, to find confirmed in the practice of the Revolution principle what I have thus far deduced only from its logic.

Tonight we make a beginning, therefore, with the history[3] of the Revolution. First, I want to submit some characteristics that I detect throughout the revolutionary era. Next, I shall explain how I divide the historical survey. Finally, in the last and major portion of this lecture I want to reflect on the Revolution in its first phase, the Preparation.

I wish to begin, as I said, with some general characteristics. This is important, for only by holding on to these can we hope, if they are correct, to sharpen our insight and keep our bearings. Because our time is limited I content myself with listing and very briefly discussing these few recurrent characteristics:

------

[3] [As an aid to the reader a Chronology of the Revolution is included at the end of this volume.]

a. The Revolution is unique in its kind.
b. It has influenced all of Christendom, directly or indirectly.
c. It destroys the foundations of law.
d. It has never been fully put into practice.
e. It has, in seeming conflict of forms, always retained its identity.
f. It has not encountered opposition except from within its own bosom.
g. It loses its power when confronted with the Gospel.

a. The Revolution is unique. In its theoretical origin and course it cannot be compared to any events of earlier times.

An exchange of regents, a reallocation of power, a change in the form of government, political conflict and religious strife have, in scope and principle, nothing in common with a social revolution whose nature is directed against every government and against every religion. They have nothing in common with a social, or more accurately, *anti-social* revolution that undermines and destroys morality and society; with an *anti-Christian* revolution whose principal idea develops into a systematic rebellion against the revealed God.

The Dutch revolt has been compared to it, as has the American revolution. In regard to the Netherlands, I simply refer you to what many, including myself, have repeatedly said about it; as regards the United States, I appeal to the noteworthy work of

Baird.[4] Nor may I acknowledge the English revolutions to be comparable to the French revolution. If you find any resemblance between the revolutions of 1688 and 1789, you should read Burke about the likeness in external appearance and the contrast in essence and principle.[5] In its principal idea the Revolution may not be compared even to 1640 and

---

[4] For the Dutch revolt, see my *Handboek*, § 131: "Freedom of Christian worship was the principal goal of the war, as suppression of the Gospel had been its principal cause. It was above all on account of religion that the struggle began; it was above all, sometimes solely, on account of religion that the struggle was continued." As for the American revolution: "The separation of the colonies from Great Britain, and the re-organisation of their respective governments, produced changes less essential than at first view might be supposed. The King, Parliament, and Justiciary of England, were superseded by the President, Congress, and Supreme Court of America, the nature of the government remaining essentially the same." Baird, *Religion in the United States of America*, p. 62. [Groen quotes the French translation by L. Burnier, *De la religion aux Etats-Unis d'Amérique,* I, 63.]

[5] "At both those periods [that of the Restoration of 1660 and that of the Revolution of 1688], the nation had lost the bond of union in their ancient edifice; they did not, however, dissolve the whole fabric. On the contrary, in both cases they regenerated the deficient part of the old constitution through the parts which were not impaired. They kept these old parts exactly as they were, that the part recovered might be suited to them. They acted by the ancient organised estates in the shape of their old organisation, and not by the organic *moleculae* of a disbanded people. At no time, perhaps, did the sovereign legislature manifest a more tender regard to that fundamental principle of British constitutional policy than at the time of the Revolution, when it deviated from the direct line of hereditary succession . . . . When the legislature altered the direction, but kept the principle, they showed that they held it inviolable." Burke, *Reflections on the Revolution in France*; in *Works*, V, 59. – Heeren rightly speaks of "the *so-called* Revolution of 1688," describing it as "a more precise establishment of

to the democratic currents and the tyranny of Cromwell's days.[6]

b. The Revolution is a European revolution, an overturning of Christendom.[7]

---

forms, which were, moreover, for the greater part old forms." *Handbuch*, p. 263. – The *Revolution* of 1688 (which was brought about by William III under his fitting motto *'Je maintiendrai'* [I shall uphold]) was in more than one respect a *Restoration*. – † "The present revolution in France seems to me to be quite of another character and description, and to bear little resemblance or analogy to any of those which have been brought about in Europe, upon principles merely political. *It is a revolution of doctrine and theoretic dogma.*" Burke, *Thoughts on French Affairs etc. etc., Written in December 1791;* in *Works*, VII, 13.

[6] "No events in history are more commonly considered parallel than the Great Rebellion in England and the French Revolution. None, with certain striking points of resemblance, are in reality more dissimilar to each other." Alison, *History of Europe*, I, 32. – † Cf. Tocqueville: "No two events could be more dissimilar than your revolution of 1640 and our great revolution of 1789 .... In my opinion they are utterly incomparable." Tocqueville to Lady Thereza Lewis, May 6, 1857; *Correspondance*, II, 381f. – Think of the words of Stahl: "The liberty of England and America breathes the spirit of the Puritans; the liberty of France breathes the spirit of the Encyclopedists and Jacobins." *Parlamentarische Reden*, p. 87f. – For an answer to the question why the English revolution was successful, read Guizot, *Pourquoi la Révolution d'Angleterre a-t-elle réussi?* And for a reply to the question so often repeated with haughty sophistication and childlike naiveté, whether we anti-revolutionaries are opposed then to each and every revolution, see my *Ter Nagedachtenis van Stahl*, p. 27 ["Of course not, we are not opposed to *every* revolution. We too know the dates 1572 and 1688. What we oppose is *the* Revolution .... the systematic overturning of ideas whereby state and society, justice and truth are founded on human opinion and arbitrariness instead of on God's ordinances"].

[7] † "This great revolution ... was prepared simultaneously

This, too, while apparent from the very nature of the case, is confirmed by attentive consideration of history. Of course, along with the identity of principle and direction, developments have differed from country to country. Some of you have asked me to what extent the succession of phases as I have sketched them *a priori* can be observed, for example, in England. This question is a fair one, since my model, if it is correct, should hold wherever the Revolution principle became dominant. Differences have arisen, however, depending on whether or not the Revolution principle did become dominant, and if so, to what degree.

Some countries, like France and, for that matter, the Netherlands, have been revolutionized; here our model is found in full. Other countries have in certain respects been brought under the *influence* of the Revolution ideas; there the situation is more complicated. In some countries the theory has continued to gain ground even though the practice, owing perhaps to events witnessed elsewhere, has skipped over, as it were, part or all of a phase: thus the revolutionary reaction became the cornerstone of policy in states where the development had hardly begun. In short, the fact that the Revolution is universal does not mean that its phases occur everywhere at the same time. Now as for England: to judge

---

throughout nearly the whole of continental Europe." Tocqueville, *L'Ancien Régime*, p. xi. "The revolutionary system is applicable to all the nations." Mallet du Pan, *Mémoires,* II, 134. The Revolution is, so to speak, *cosmopolitan.*

from the modifications the revolutionary ideas have undergone in the minds of many of her statesmen, England has already reached a period of discouragement and decrepitude even though her state and society have not been turned upside down. The struggle against French Jacobinism temporarily arrested the logical progress of the Revolution. Nevertheless, the phase of preparation did resume its course later: and so inner decay is stirring even now in England. No longer is there a steady hand to maintain the traditional public law. Yet in the meantime, as long as her constitution remains in force England will continue to be rich in privileges and inequalities, the presence of which will continue to exacerbate the revolutionary mind. Even England can therefore be said to be lingering on the threshold of the upheaval.[8]

c. The Revolution doctrine undermines and destroys the foundations of law.

Wherever the Revolution has been at work it has become apparent that it considers law to be mere convention, a product of the human will. Law, thus ever changeable in its origin, is delivered up to arbitrariness. Lawfulness is replaced by "legality," legitimacy by "the legal order."[9]

---

[8] † Since 1847 England, as appears from her domestic and foreign politics, has come even closer.

[9] † "The opposite of popular sovereignty, and therefore the basic truth of politics, is *the principle of legitimacy*, that is, of the authority of the existing order of law and of government .... The concept of legitimacy and of government from God is *anything but*

As you know, some people think I belong to a coterie of Parisian legitimists or at least sympathize with them.[10] That fact will not prevent my expressing full agreement with the principle of legitimacy as expressed in the following lines:

There are sacred, inviolable, legitimate matters which, placed under the aegis of justice universally recognized, must never be changed and may not be sacrificed by any human authority. This is the principle of legitimacy in its highest universality.

There is no universal justice. Nothing is sacred, inviolable, legitimate. All laws may be changed at the pleasure of the sovereign, and the sovereign is he who is the strongest. All rights may be sacrificed to the general welfare, and the general welfare is that which it pleases us so to call. There you have the principle of illegitimacy, or of the Revolution, in all its colossal scope.[11]

d. The revolutionary theory was never realized in full.

This thesis is supported by history without exception. In 1816 Haller wrote about the experiments in France and elsewhere: "In reality there was no social contract, no sovereignty of the people, no separation of powers, but only a struggle of parties to take possession of the supreme power." And what

---

absolutistic. Exactly the opposite." Stahl, *Die Revolution und die constitutionelle Monarchie*, pp. 18, 20. See also my *Grondwetherziening*, pp. 338ff, 472.

[10] Cf. above, p. 000.

[11] *Journal des débats*, 1819.

could be said in 1816 is as undeniable in 1846: "Every attempt that was launched to put the philosophical system into practice failed utterly." The theory was never realized because realization was an impossibility. "It failed because it *had* to fail; because the system itself is false, impracticable and contrary to reason; and because the omnipotent force of nature resists its execution."[12]

But, it is countered, this failure was caused by deviations or excessiveness; by the unripeness of the peoples; by an unhappy conjunction of circumstances; by personal errors and missteps.

There was no deviation or excessiveness, but application. The application was forced through without regard to humanity, true; but always along the projected path. In fact, the horrible experiment never even neared the summit, or rather, the abyss of its pure and full development. "It cannot be alleged," writes Haller,

that principles are stretched too far or that they are exceeded or ill applied when the results are derived rigorously from the premises. If precepts are sound, they, like the laws of nature, must the more firmly establish and authenticate themselves by

---

[12] Haller, *Restauration*, I, 332, 321, 334f. — † "The great sign and judgment on the Revolution theory is that its constitutions not only lacked durability, but that almost all of them could not even be brought to realization. Not a single constitution of France has, to use the celebrated expression, become a truth." Stahl, *Philosophie des Rechts*, III, 364. ["become a truth": an allusion to the expression 'la charte-vérité'; see below, p. 000n0. *Note by H. Smitskamp.*]

their results and effects. No, it is not true that these principles were exceeded; rather, everything failed because these principles are false. It would in fact be easy to prove that precisely the most disastrous consequences, which made more than one partisan of the system shudder, flowed all too rigorously from the principles, and that still many more evils and horrors would have resulted if man's heart and natural sentiments, less corrupt than the prevailing systems, had not from time to time revolted against the errors of the mind to arrest their application.[13]

The peoples, it is said, were not ripe. — Singular pretence! Amid the trumpet sound of progress and enlightenment one would rather have thought of the adage, "Now or never! " If this highly enlightened generation, which lectures mankind, be not ripe, when then, pray tell, will the peoples be ripe? Besides, this pretext is hardly in keeping with what we have been told about the truth of the principle and the excellence of the forms deriving from it. You depict to me a theory which promises the perfection of man in state and society, and when I rejoice and when I desire the realization of the promise, you point toward a distant future, and you demand that the fruit, in order to benefit from the warming rays, be ripe beforehand. I thought your new-fashioned sunshine was to bask it to ripeness!

Writes Rousseau: "If there were a nation of gods, it would govern itself democratically. So perfect

---
[13] Haller, *Restauration*, I, 326f.

a government is unsuited to man."[14] I would sooner say: so *imperfect* a government. The excellence of a doctrine, after all, is proportional to the difficulties it surmounts. Look at the doctrine we Christians profess. In the experimental verification of the words, "When we were dead in sins, He hath quickened us together with Christ,"[15] in the burgeoning and blossoming of morality on the soil of evangelical doctrine, lies the abiding proof of divine power. But when earthly wisdom reverses the order and says, "Let the people first be good and then I shall undertake their improvement; let them first be alive and then I shall make them live and let the fruit of my lessons be seen"—then we recognize this to be a confession of impotence and a contradiction of the indicated prospect. Then we say the more boldly: never shall the peoples be ripe enough to find happiness by this doctrine, since its very nature is pernicious.

But in circumstances or in persons, it is asserted, lie cause and fault. In this manner, through evasions of all sorts, the uniqueness of the root is ignored. With equal right one could blame the aridity of the soil, the instability of the weather, the multiplication of vermin or the incompetence of the vinedresser for the fact that one cannot gather grapes from thorns or figs from thistles. With equal right one could praise

---

[14] Rousseau, *Du contrat social*; in *Oeuvres*, II, 88. Cf. above, p. 000n.

[15] Eph. 2:5.

the qualities of a tree from which none but deadly fruits were ever picked. One complains about the circumstances even when all the circumstances were favourable. One complains about the deviations and aberrations of men and forgets that, under the influence of the Revolution ideas, free choice is restricted to the variety of ways that lead astray.

e. Everywhere the Revolution principle retains its identity.

Men are infatuated with an anarchy that is called liberty; or with an arbitrariness that boasts of being a strong and brilliant administration; or with the representative institutions of liberalism that conceal the vain pursuit of an unattainable equilibrium. Jacobinism, Bonapartism, Constitutionalism[16] —all are branches of the same tree, or rather, fresh shoots on the same branch: continuations of the line which the Revolution principle has projected for itself in the form (to use Goethe's expression) of a *spiral*, a path of self-perfection. They are not three political philosophies, but one and the same tripartite philosophy.[17]

---

[16] † "Constitutional monarchy, in its true meaning, is *moral progress.*" Stahl, *Die gegenwärtige Parteien*, p. 173. Constitutional monarchy has nothing in common with Constitutionalism: the doctrine of the separation of powers and checks and balances, in which kingship dissolves into *the executive power.*

[17] "What characterizes the prevailing attitude of European man even today is the persistent belief in an *absolute State* which stands above every existing law. The three main forms, Republicanism,

It seems to me that this observation sheds a great deal of light, not only on the character of events, but also on the conduct of persons.

We are irritated by the chameleonic careers of those who started out as Jacobins, then turned Bonapartist, and ended up opposing every lawful administration. We are irritated, and rightly so, when criminal passion, ambition and egoism manage to fold themselves to fit the fashion:

In times of revolution there always appears a race of perverse beings to whom evil is pleasing and who love it for its own sake. Only on top of ruins are they able to breathe freely; and when they are suffered to have power, crime streams from

---

Constitutionalism and Imperialism, are in essence based on the same principles, however different their external appearances may be. Whenever it was a question of fighting the Truth, therefore, the followers of the three schools always co-operated, however vehemently they fought each other after the victory." *Berliner politisches Wochenblatt*. 1832, p. 222. − † About Goethe's image of the spiral, see my *Proeve*, p. 55 ["How could a system belied by both history and Scripture [i.e., the doctrine of perfectibility] have become so popular? There was a need for coherence and unity, which unbelief could meet in no other way. . . . Improvement, real or imaginary, was enlarged upon without any examination of its source (whether it was from man or from God, through human impulse or through higher power). Stagnation and regression were purported to be roundabout ways of progress, detours necessary to reach the goal. (Madame de Stael says, 'On the perfectibility of the human mind Goethe has spoken a word full of wisdom: "*It is always advancing, but in a spiral line*." ' Given this escape, there is no historical evidence that could ever bring these defenders of perfectibility to silence.) Thus the whole of history was distorted in an arbitrarily chosen form. This doctrine penetrated wherever men had no decent knowledge of either history or Scripture . . ."].

their souls as lava from the crater. Others, occupied solely with their personal interest and indifferent to everything else, foment disorder for the purpose of creating opportunities favourable to their own profit. They sell themselves to anyone who will pay them. Today they are found in revolutionary clubs demanding the heads of kings; tomorrow they will be seen kneeling at the feet of the basest tyrant, adoring his whims and justifying his crimes.[18]

Quite so, but this character sketch by Lamennais is not applicable in all cases. There have been those whose convictions did indeed keep pace with the changes in the practice of the Revolution but who were, nevertheless, always at work with the same zeal for the same object: the realization of the revolutionary theory.

We are offended by many a statesman whose liberalism shone outside the government but who, having entered the government himself, excelled in arbitrariness. We are offended; and, I repeat, sometimes not unjustly so. Sometimes a lack of honesty and good faith is unmistakable. However, we could go too far with such suspicions and withhold respect from men who deserve it. For at least in some of the instances in which their conduct appears irresponsible and treacherous these ever useful instruments of the Revolution doctrine were only being faithful to the theory, which throughout all its metamorphoses might have disappointed them in its results but never in its promises.

---

[18] Lamennais, *Oeuvres complètes,* II, 247.

We are indignant with those who were subservient with the same readiness to all governments and never scrupled to take an oath or accept a distinguished or profitable office. We are indignant; and here again I say, the many instances in which men were motivated by self-interest and ambition justify our indignation. But still, let us not lose sight of the altered conceptions of state and government. It was always a revolutionary state that survived and lived on. The various revolutions were but transfers of revolutionary power, in this sense, that each administration in turn was recognized as the result of the rightly omnipotent will of the majority. Thus on this view the government was not, as formerly, a monarch or a sovereign corporation with whose independent existence the state itself stands or falls. Rather, the government was a passing embodiment of the state, a transient manifestation of the sovereign people, designed to be but the servant of the nation, the mandatary of the country. Therefore supporting or opposing a government had become a question centering on persons, a question that was settled in the name of the Public as soon as the stronger Party had prevailed. Consequently, far from a praiseworthy loyalty, attachment to a banished government had become a prejudice, and perhaps high treason.[19] Thus Talleyrand used to argue that in serving and

---

[19] † *Fatherland* and *nation* are identified with the state, with a government. One's *country* then consists in "the crushing unity of the *central power* enthroned as the symbol of *national unity*." Guizot,

abandoning each government he had always remained loyal to his country and consistent with himself.[20]

Like all of that grand generation to which he belonged, Talleyrand sincerely loved his fatherland and never lost his fondness for the ideas of his youth and the principles of 1789; they stayed with him through all vicissitudes of events and of fortune. Without any shame he would talk about the governments he had served and deserted. He used to say that he had not served the governments but the country, under the political institution which seemed to him at the moment to be the most suitable; and that he had never wanted to sacrifice

---

Mémoires, III, 217 (emphasis added). This confusion of concepts gradually led to seeing the fatherland in every successfully established regime (cf. above, pp. 00f, 000f). Thus the oath became a commitment merely to the form in which the will of the people happened to be organized at any moment; hence loyalty to any fallen government, even to the most native dynasty, became narrow-minded delinquency and dereliction of duty.

[20] [Charles Maurice de Talleyrand-Périgord (1754-1838), a consumer of opportunities, intrigued to serve and desert as many mortal men and causes as seemed to him to be required. He first played a role in the Revolution and then held high offices under Napoleon, Louis XVIII and Louis Philippe. In 1789/90 he was among the first prelates to advocate the confiscation of church lands for the benefit of the nation and to agree to the civil constitution of the clergy. After a brief political exile spent in America, he served as foreign minister under the Directory, but with provisional loyalty. He helped Napoleon to power when his star was rising, but left him when his days seemed numbered. He abetted the restoration of the Bourbons, whom he represented on behalf of France at the Congress of Vienna, but later turned up among the opposition of the liberal left and helped prepare the Orleanist coup of 1830. Although Talleyrand's motives have been subjected to much speculation, his substantial achievements as a statesman are a matter of record.]

the interest of France to the interest of anyone in power. . . .[21]

Apart from the question whether or not the excuse is really applicable to the cunning egotist who thus systematized it, it cannot be doubted that this typically revolutionary view had great influence on the actions of many.

f. The history of the Revolution will also bear out the following thesis, to which I attach special importance: amid much controversy issue was never taken with the essence of the Revolution as such.

Many endeavours that were looked upon as such were not anti-revolutionary at all. There was no war save civil and fratricidal war, a steady struggle of the revolutionaries among themselves. The false theory was resisted in its development, never attacked at its origin and root.[22] Not even by the scholars. Haller writes:

---

[21] Mignet, *Etudes et portraits politiques,* I, 159.

[22] † Cf. my *Verspreide Geschriften*, I, 124-134 [reprinted from *Nederlandsche Gedachten* (Sept. 27 - Nov. 19, 1831): "Chief cause of the many revolutions ravaging the civilized world is the false philosophy of which unbelief is the source and eternal strife the ineluctable outcome. This baleful doctrine must be attacked in its origin, in the principle from which it stems. Has this been done? Hardly. It has been done neither in 1789 nor in 1815 nor in 1830. There has been no conflict about the doctrine but only about the degree of development and the manner and timeliness of application. . . . Although the doctrine was resisted in many ways as it unfolded in history, no one ever struck at the heart of it: the principle was accepted and the consequences rejected, even though the principle was false and the consequences correct"].

Out of respect for the truth it ought to be said that the attacks by the scholars were never sufficiently strong or thorough and that they lacked especially the solid and systematic form necessary to oppose the error. The same lack seems to me to be common to the numerous authors who during the French revolution combatted either the revolution itself or its principles and consequences. Employing only the weapons of history against the philosophical system, some demonstrated that the social contract had never existed; yet they failed to demonstrate that it *could* not and *ought* not to exist. Others attacked only the dangerous consequences, not the principles themselves; the ruinous fruits, not the root of the error. Finally, they proved incapable of building up a rival system which would be satisfying in all respects and adequate for explaining, in a legitimate and thorough fashion, the origin, nature and exercise of sovereign authority. They failed to present things in the way they really are, in their true aspect. They warned against the poison but failed to offer an efficacious antidote.[23]

They acted like the incompetent physician who fights the symptoms but does not know the cause of the disease.

g. I called this last point important among other reasons because it reassures us concerning the supposed insurmountability of the error. For, if unbelief is the principle, the remedy lies in belief, in faith.

There is no reason for despondency so long as

---

[23] Haller, *Restauration*, I, 339.

the foolproof cure has not been tried and is still available. What can be learned from the experience of the revolutionary era? That man, without God, even with the circumstances in his favour, can do nothing but work his own destruction. Man must break out of the vicious revolutionary circle; he must turn to God whose truth alone can resist the power of the lie. Should anyone consider this momentous lesson of history to be more sentimental lament than advice for politics, he is forgetting that the power of the Gospel to effect order and freedom and prosperity has been substantiated by world history. Let him bear in mind that whatever is useful and beneficial to man is promoted by the fear of God and thwarted by the denial of God. He should bear in mind especially that the revolutionary theory was an unfolding of the germ of unbelief, and that the poisonous plant which was cultivated by apostasy from the faith will wilt and choke in the atmosphere of a revival of the faith.

To these characteristics of the history of the Revolution let me now join *the arbitrariness of revolutionary state authority*, which I discussed at the end of the previous lecture. The revolutionary state, in which the General Will and the government are bundled together, has as its foundational principle that fateful error whose origins we have found in the perversion of constitutional law and in the writings of Machiavellians and Monarchomachs, the error which we later discovered to be inseparable from the revolutionary theory: the error of assuming an original liberty and equality, with everything that this entails. This error forms the axis around which the wheels of the state machinery turn. The machinery may be operated by various regimes with greater or lesser amounts of energy for the purpose of attaining various ends in keeping with the flux of circumstances and the diversity of viewpoints and sympathies. Structurally and operationally, however, the machinery itself remains unchanged, as well after 1813 as after 1789, as well after 1840 as after 1830. The result, then—whether it be under tyrants or benevolent rulers, representatives who resist or who yield, a democratic or an autocratic regime—is that the most essential liberties, the most cherished memories and the most sacred trusts of the nation will be respected, protected, tolerated and spared only insofar as they can be fitted and subjected to the demands of the state, that is, to the demands of those who happen directly or indirectly to run the government. This I have called *the despotism of the revolutionary state.*

Proceeding now to the historical survey, I must indicate how I plan to divide it. It seems to me that the simplest division is given in the five phases outlined last time in connection with the purely logical course of the Revolution ideas: Preparation (till 1789), Development (1789-1794), Reaction (1794-1813), Renewed Experimentation (1813-1830), and Despondent Resignation (since 1830).

Quite often I shall have to direct your attention

almost exclusively to France. There more than anywhere else the disease had unimpeded course. For this
very reason, however, I must warn once more against
considering the Revolution a *national* disease to be
explained solely or especially from the frivolous
nature of the *French.*[24] To the contrary, the sickness
was more epidemic than contagious. For a long time
there had been turbulence and agitation everywhere.
If the fire opened an outlet for itself in France, we
may not forget that the whole European ground was
volcanic.[25] Even the prolonged superiority of French
arms must for the larger part be explained from the
universality of the revolutionary corruption: resistance against the Franco-revolutionary violence was
vain because hatred of France was overshadowed by
love for the experiment begun on French soil. The

---

[24] † Take, for example, the following interpretation: "The
French revolution, which has always been considered a universal event
in world history (even Hegel committed that error), was at bottom a
fact quite peculiar to France. It was a Gallic fact; it was the result, if I
may venture to say so, of that *vanity* which enables the Gaul to put up
with anything except inequality of social rank; and of that absolute
logic which leads him to reform society after an abstract model,
without taking history or sacred rights into account." Thus explains
Ernest Renan, in an article in the *Revue des deux mondes*, 28 (1858),
XIV, 519 [emphasis added]. Amusing though he may be, Renan is
wrong. Logic and the passions come into play to effectuate the false
doctrine only after men have let go of the principles that are true. See
also above, p. 000n.

[25] † As late as 1848 Tocqueville writes: "We are standing in the
midst of a general revolution of the civilized peoples, and I believe that
in the long run not one of them shall escape it." *Oeuvres complètes*, VI,
141. "There is but *one* revolution, which is still raging, and which will
not be finished for a long time." *Ibid.*, VII, 198.

European revolution found its epitome in the French one. The Revolution is not to be ascribed to the French nation: it was the work of a faction, of a sect, of a philosophical school which used the irresistible powers of centralized government to bring the nation—and every nation in proportion as it was being revolutionized—under the yoke of the successive personifications of its principle.[26]

Since the French revolution will thus naturally constitute an important part of the lectures that are to follow, I should like briefly to note with you the value of the chief works on the subject. Certainly the standpoint of most authors on the French revolution has been derived from the revolutionary ideas themselves, so that with respect to their works we must watch carefully for errors of judgment related to principles we reject. For a critical survey of the literature, even if I were able, I lack the time. With respect to a few works, however, a short comment will not be amiss if taken in connection with what I said in the second lecture about several anti-revolutionary books.

The works of Thiers and Mignet, excellent in form, the one as a running account, the other as a compact sketch,[27] go so far as to defend the revolution even in its horrors—horrors which, accord-

---

[26] "Since 1789 hardly any of the crises that have occurred in France were desired by the nation." Madame de Stael, *Considérations*, II, 57. — † Always and everywhere the *Nation* was the slave of the spokesmen of the *Sovereign People*.

[27] A. Thiers, *Histoire de la révolution française* (2nd ed.; 10

ing to these men, were prerequisite to its triumph; meanwhile they ignore or twist the arguments and documentary evidence of the opposing party.[28] Many years ago Necker and Madame de Stael[29] were adjudged the best by Heeren;[30] perhaps they still

---

vols.; Liège, 1828-29). F.-A. Mignet, *Histoire de la révolution française, depuis 1789 jusqu'en 1814* (5th ed.; 2 vols.; Paris, 1833).

[28] A very extensive review of the works of Thiers [by J.W. Croker] in the *Quarterly Review*, vol. 76 (1845), pp. 521-583, is quite successful in convincing the reader of what is said in the opening words: "In the fourteen Octavo Volumes of his Histories there is not one single page, hardly one line, of sincere and unadulterated truth." – The publication of Thiers' history of the French revolution was "a bookseller's speculation on the state of political parties in France; a branch of the general conspiracy against the elder Bourbons; a paradoxical apology for the old Revolution, and a covert provocation to a new one." – "Thiers' portrait flatters the Revolution by altering the details; Mignet's coarser and colourless hand falsifies the outline." – † This most noteworthy review article has since appeared in J.W. Croker, *Essays on the Early Period of the French Revolution* (London, 1857). No one, perhaps, has studied the events and the characters of the French revolution from 1789 to 1794 with as much precision as this too little known Englishman, a member of Parliament, of whom Guizot testifies: "Of all the champions of old English Toryism . . . he is the one who has best made me see and understand his party . . . . From my conversations with him I have learned much about the state of British society and the history of his times." *Mémoires*, V, 164f. – [Thiers' *Histoire de la révolution française*, first published from 1823 to 1827, did indeed serve as an additional weapon in the arsenal of the liberal opposition against the Bourbons; cf. below, pp. 000f. *Note by H. Smitskamp.*]

[29] Jacques Necker, *De la révolution française* (2 vols.; Paris, 1797). Madame la baronne de Stael [= Anne-Louise-Germaine Necker], *Considérations sur les principaux événemens de la révolution françoise* (3 vols.; Paris, 1818).

[30] "Among the flood of French writings those of Necker and his intelligent daughter lead the list." Heeren, *Handbuch*, p. 585.

rank among the best, provided we remember that political prejudice cramps even genius and that in both father and daughter a very strong tinge of Anglomania is unmistakably present. Wachmuth's *History of France in the Revolution Era,*[31] with its stamp of faint liberalism, is important for its accuracy and vividness, at least up to the Consulate; the Restoration, on the other hand, he treats with a partiality resembling satire and a superficiality resembling the chronicle in the back of an almanac. Alison's *History of Europe*[32] excels in scholarship and impartiality, in lofty reflection from the perspectives of religion, morality and justice—although my objection is that the author confuses the revolution too much with a conflict about a democratic form of government. Schlosser's *History of the Eighteenth Century,*[33] to judge from the volumes that have appeared to date, can be reckoned among the more important contributions to the study of the Revolution, although his lack of acquaintance with the spirit and power of the Gospel betrays itself in faulty insights and acrid judgments.[34]

---

[31] Wilhelm Wachsmuth, *Geschichte Frankreichs im Revolutions-zeitalter* (4 vols.; Hamburg, 1840-44), in the series *Geschichte der europäischen Staaten* edited by A.H.L. Heeren and F.A. Ukert.

[32] Archibald Alison, *History of Europe from the Commencement of the French Revolution in 1789 to the Restoration of the Bourbons in 1815* (5 vols.; Paris, 1841 - 42).

[33] Friedrich Christoph Schlosser, *Geschichte des achtzehnten Jahrhunderts und des neunzehnten bis zum Sturz des französischen Kaiserreichs* (Heidelberg, 1836-   ).

[34] † As I wrote in the *Archives,* VII, p. xlv: "Mr. Schlosser

Many another book I could place on the table.[35] But it is high time that I spend our remaining moments in showing you the Preparation of the Revolution in the period preceding 1789.

The Preparation of the Revolution was twofold, depending on whether we consider Europe in general or France in particular. Let us first retrace how in Europe as a whole the Revolution spirit gained

---

asserts that the historical side is the Gospel's weak side (thus the truth must have weak sides, or else the Gospel is not the truth). We, on the other hand, believe that until the end of time the destiny of mankind will be governed by the destiny of the Church of Christ as revealed in Scripture."

[35] † See also above, in the Preface, where I mention the works of Lamartine and Louis Blanc. Croker's judgment of Lamartine's historical critique (as far as I know, he does not speak anywhere about Louis Blanc's) is very unfavourable. Writes Croker, "All through his history he embroiders his narrative with numerous anecdotes, for which he gives and for which my tolerably extensive reading of revolutionary history supplies no authority. Of the inaccuracies and, in fact, the falsehood of many of these anecdotes we have abundant and indisputable evidence." *Essays*, p. 428. – Since the first edition of this book in 1847, there have appeared numerous publications (a library by itself) on the French revolution. I mention only J. Mallet du Pan, *Mémoires et correspondance pour servir à l'histoire de la révolution française,* collected and edited by A. Sayous (2 vols.; Paris, 1851), an important contribution from the legacy of this outstanding anti-revolutionary publicist; Heinrich von Sybel, *Geschichte der Revolutionszeit von 1789 bis 1795* (1853; 2nd ed., 3 vols., Düsseldorf, 1859-60); and, last but not least, the invaluable labour of Alexis de Tocqueville in *L'Ancien Régime et la Révolution* (Paris, 1856) and especially in the numerous fragments from his, alas unfinished, reflections on the revolution itself (1789-1815) [in *Oeuvres complètes*, VIII (1865): *Mélanges, fragments historiques et notes, sur l'Ancien Régime, la Révolution, et l'Empire.*]

ground, and then how especially in France, long before 1789, an upheaval of the state became inevitable.

About Europe I shall be brief. I lack the talent for giving a history of the eighteenth century in a quarter of an hour. Besides, the entire content of these lectures is related, directly or indirectly, to this subject. From what has been noted earlier about the nature of both the historical constititional law and the revolutionary constitutional law, it is evident immediately that if the latter should ever prevail over the former, the preparation and inception of an immense revolution would necessarily follow. That the victory of the latter is equal to the destruction of the former follows from the nature of the case. I have to prove only one thing: that the false theory, pregnant with so many calamities, in fact did enter the field, did gain the ascendancy, and did achieve dominion. But, I ask you, who of us is ignorant of this? It is visible everywhere and in everything.

With the tree of life planted once more in the European soil by the Reformation all but dead, the ground was ready to receive the deadly seed. Theology, political theory, literature and education: all these were soon permeated by the new doctrine. This leaven leavened the whole lump. At the outbreak of the French revolution virtually all of Europe was ripe for upheaval. Many a prelude was to be observed in lesser states. Practically everywhere the majority of those who excelled in capability and nobility of spirit were revolution-minded.[36] Generally applicable is what Madame de Stael writes of the French revolution: "Everything and nothing is to be blamed for the revolution: each year of the century led towards it along all roads."[37]

If, however, you would like me to discuss at least one feature of the European physiognomy, then I select the mode of thinking and acting of the monarchs. Practically all of them believed in the new philosophy, and their faithful obedience to its precepts reveals that this belief was a sincere and living faith. Strange though this may seem, it can be explained from the general enthusiasm in which some were caught up even against their own interests; and from the bait which concealed from them the barbs of the false ideas: that is, the attractive notion that their personal, independent authority was not yet half so great as the power which they would be able to

---

[36] "A new era seemed to have dawned upon the world. . . . It was not merely the factious, the restless, and the ambitious, who entertained these opinions, they were shared by many of the best and wisest of men; and in England it might with truth be said what an eloquent historian ([C.G.G.] Botta) has observed of Europe in general, that the friends of the French revolution comprised at that period the most enlightened and generous of the community." Alison, *History,* I, 260. – † "Underneath all great movements that agitate the spirits, hidden intrigues are always found. They form as it were the substratum of revolutions. But . . . the change in ideas which ended in changing the facts was enacted in broad daylight by the joint efforts of all–authors, nobles, and princes, all abandoning the old society without knowing what society they were entering." Tocqueville to the Count of Gircourt, June 14, 1852; *Correspondance,* II, 187.

[37] Madame de Stael, *Considérations,* I, 88.

derive, whether by sly calculation or in good faith, from the theory of revolutionary state omnipotence.

Important here are the observations made about this matter by Haller. The *philosophes*, or sophists, were on confidential terms with the world's great:

It is well known that in Spain the dukes of Aranda, Alva and Villa Hermosa, ministers of the King; in Portugal the all too famous Pombal; and in Italy several great lords, were counted among the pupils and patrons of the French sophists. King Christian VII of Denmark; Gustavus III of Sweden, since fallen by the assassin's lead, and before him his mother Ulrica; King Stanislas Poniatowski of Poland; and Empress Catherine II of Russia[38] had corresponded privately with the French philosophers and expressed complete agreement, if not with their political, then at least with their anti-religious dogmas.[39]

Soon they were also won over to their view of the state. The prospect of incalculable gain was alluring.

They managed [Haller observes] to present the new philosophical principles to the sovereigns as being suitable for enlarging their power and for liberating them from all the limitations which their authority had hitherto encountered in natural justice and positive conventions. Although on the one hand it is fine and pleasant to be lord and master and to

---

[38] [These rulers and statesmen of the second half of the eighteenth century, known as the "enlightened despots," wanted to apply the ideas of the Enlightenment while preserving their absolute power, in accordance with the motto: 'Everything *for* the people, nothing *by* the people.' *Note by H. Smitskamp.*]

[39] Haller, *Restauration*, I, 145.

command in one's own name by virtue of one's own right, on the other hand it is also profitable sometimes to appear as the highest *functionary* or employee; to unite the personal with the delegated authority; and, in case of need, to act by virtue of a so-called mandate which no one may ever criticize or revoke. The employee is paid: the presumed will of his master constitutes an ever ready excuse for all the servant's actions. Self-interest and injustices of all kinds are covered with the cloak called *the happiness of the people*. The moment the rulers pass themselves off as the first officials of the nation, their wars become national wars, their debts national debts, their needs state needs. Conscription, arbitrary taxes and every other kind of forced service are quite conveniently justified by the concepts of a public establishment and of the sovereignty of the people. Private rights and agreements made with individuals or corporations no longer have any value the moment everything must be subservient to the alleged ends of the state, to the interest of the majority, or to the presumed will of the people, which is even presented as the source of all justice.

That is the siren song with which credulous monarchs were seduced and plunged into the abyss. But the flatterers knew better than to show them the opposite side of these principles, according to which an employee may also be discharged, dismissed, or have his salary reduced. Much less did they tell them that the people, that imaginary sovereign, would naturally come to desire to give orders to its servants; to decide on war and peace; in a word, to govern—directly or otherwise—all affairs, which were said to be its own affairs anyway . . . . Thus it can be explained how our day has witnessed powerful princes, led astray by the principles of the philosophic constitutional law, themselves undermining the foundation of their authority and digging the abyss which was to swallow them.[40]

Later perhaps we shall have the opportunity to show the altered ideas about international law: at present our concern is only with domestic government. The revolutionary phraseology became common. As Haller notes:

The political system of the philosophers, the unnatural idea of an authority deriving from the people, was spread far and wide during the last twenty years of the eighteenth century. It took root in almost every brain. It predominated almost without exception in literary as well as in popular writings. Here and there, with long intervals, some words of truth were still to be heard, spoken weakly and timidly as by a voice expiring in the wilderness. The parlance of the new system gradually penetrated even into the style of the chancelleries, where, if anywhere, the former expressions and appellations, which had been derived from nature, should have been preserved with the most devoted respect. Instead of this ancient paternal language, full of strength and cordiality, impregnated with the consciousness of one's own rights and of others' rights, there was to be heard in the royal laws and ordinances published during the last thirty years of the eighteenth century talk only of civil association, of authority delegated by the people, of legislative and executive powers, of servants of the state or of public functionaries, of state finances, of state goods, of the purpose of government, of the destiny of mankind, of citizens of the state, of constitutions and organizations, of the obligations of the sovereign, of the rights of the people, and so

---

[40] *Ibid.*, I, 200-202.

on—expressions and locutions which, having originated in the schools of the modern philosophy, had of necessity to aggravate the general confusion of ideas and to erase even the memory of the former correct relations.[41]

Words bring about deeds. Once the monarchs were construed to be heads of a state defined—according to a theory in which they too concurred—by the absoluteness of popular sovereignty, they were no longer held back by any sacredness of vested rights or historic liberties but went to work with revolutionary omnipotence as the crowned deputies of the Sovereign People. General regularization, centralization and codification became the order of the day. Despotism, unlawful and odious when exercised in one's own name, now masqueraded as duty and benevolence practised in the name of liberty and enlightenment and for the sake of the common good.

I could sketch some principal figures in this contest. Among the Portuguese we find Pombal, highly lauded because he was an enemy of the clergy, and of whom even Schlosser testifies that, despite his philosophical reforms, he deserves to be no less abhorred than a Danton or a Marat.[42] In Russia there was the adulterous murderess,[43] hailed by her Parisian friends as the Semiramis of the North,

---

[41] *Ibid.*, I, 254.

[42] "The horrible retaliation of Pombal would alone have sufficed to make him and his philosophical reforms as detestable as a Danton or a Marat." Schlosser, *Geschichte,* III, 29.

[43] [The reference is to Czarina Catherine II.]

perhaps among other reasons because she had, shall we say the crafty or the droll, whim to convoke in Moscow an assembly from all classes, from all tongues, from all religions, for the forming of a General Code of Law: an assembly which indeed convened; which received in the name of the empress an *Instruction*, a wretched concoction of the wisdom of Montesquieu and Rousseau;[44] and which left behind no sign of life except the appointment of fifteen committees for constitution, finances, military affairs, legislation, and so forth: committees which after seven years of labour also returned home, having accomplished nothing. In Prussia we have Frederick II who, captivated by philosophy and a friend of philosophers, gave a firm boost to the advancement of liberalism (though he was evidently endowed with plenty of anti-philosophical energy whenever his prerogative was at stake). His successor, Frederick William II, a toy of Illuminists[45] and Jacobins, scarcely on the throne, thought to make his people happy overnight by issuing a general code of law in

---

[44] "The pitiful hodgepodge of a dabbler who, under the name of the empress, wanted to dish up and implement a wisdom borrowed from Montesquieu and Rousseau." Haller, *Restauration,* I, 120. — In this *Instruction of Her Imperial Majesty to the Commissioners for Composing a New Code of Laws* (St. Petersburgh, 1767) one reads [in § 158]: "A Code containing all the Laws must be a book of average size which, like the Catechism, may be purchased at a modest price and be learnt by heart." Meanwhile, "notice that the *Instruction* alone, comprising a kind of table of contents, numbers close to three hundred pages." Haller, *ibid.,* I, 211.

[45] [For the Illuminists, see above, p. 000f.]

four parts, according to the fashion of philosophy. In Austria we see Joseph II, a true apprentice of philosophy; a ruler who meant well, who thought well of his own ideas, who was convinced of the beneficial tendency of the unbelieving philosophy; who, in his charitable intent to make others happy, prescribed and by force of arms imposed what was for himself—and therefore for everyone, of course? — quite Christian and religious enough; who saw in the destruction of the estates and the demolition of ancient institutions the first condition for uplifting society; who thought he could throw all ethnic peculiarities and laws and customs into the revolutionary melting pot; who finally, having come into the possession, at his accession, of countries prosperous and thriving, left them behind after a few short years in confusion, civil war and defection; so that the despotic project-maker's death came as a message of universal relief, the only possible remedy in the nick of time.[46]

---

[46] † "We see the crowned 'friend of man,' as his contemporaries fondly called him, not only destroy arbitrarily those privileges of nobility and clergy detrimental to the common interest, but also attack with brute force the deepest foundations of human life: religion, language, and love for one's native soil." Sybel, *Geschichte*, I, 165. — The doctrine of the sovereignty of the People was confessed by everyone who flattered himself that he could remain the master, or the organ, of the Sovereign; cf. my *Verscheidenheden*, pp. 104ff ["Frederick II . . . was certainly in favour of popular sovereignty, provided he would remain master of the Sovereign. He was happy to be the servant of the collective lord, provided this Sovereign . . . would equal the do-nothing kings of mediaeval times and his own service the servitude of a

Enough said to recall that the rulers and magistrates in almost every country were found "at the head of the movement." Napoleon once made the remark (which for that matter is obvious to any attentive observer) that "a revolution in France is always, sooner or later, followed by a revolution in Europe."[47] Naturally, for even in the days of its preparation the movement was European, so that in some places, for example in the Netherlands,[48] the hardly repressed outbreak even preceded 1789.

I still have to prove more specifically that the *French* revolution had been in preparation for a long

---

Mayor of the Palace. . . . The doctrine of popular sovereignty was ratified by everyone who fancied he could be the organ of the Sovereign People"]. — Nor were the monarchs alone guilty; even in those days the rulers but "faithfully represented their times." *Ibid.*, p. 330.

[47] Quoted in Alison, *History,* I, 257. — † Or, as Metternich puts it: "When France has a cold, Europe sneezes."

[48] [Reference to the events of 1786-87, when the Patriot movement for democratic reform was forcibly quelled after it had resorted to arms. By 1785, as the result of an uneasy alliance between the aristocratic regents who were traditionally jealous of the influence of the House of Orange and the bourgeois Patriots whose spokesmen preached popular sovereignty, the Prince of Orange had been deprived of many of his powers as Stadtholder. With the Dutch Republic divided into regents, democrats and orangists, civil war seemed imminent. However, in 1787 the Prince's wife, Wilhelmina, with the aid of her brother the king of Prussia who was backed by English diplomatic guarantees against France, succeeded in chastening the regents, dispersing the various Patriot free corps, and disbanding the Patriot societies, whose leaders then fled to France. The curtailments to the office of Stadtholder were removed and a semblance of order restored. See also below, p. 000.]

time. Is this not a foregone conclusion? After what has been said about Europe there is no reason to suppose that France was an exception. I could almost content myself with quoting Madame de Stael's observation about the coming of the revolution in France: "All words and all actions, all virtues and all passions, all sentiments and all vanities, the public spirit and the fashion tended equally toward the same goal."[49]

Nevertheless some elaboration of my own views on the question does not seem superfluous. It is true, the narrowmindedness that confused occasion and cause has somewhat passed. No longer do authors attribute the fall of the French monarchy to its financial plight. Many now recognize the truth of the statement with which Madame de Stael opens her work: "The French revolution marks one of the great epochs of the social order. Those who consider it an accidental event have paid attention neither to the past nor to the future. They have mistaken the actors for the play, and to satisfy their prejudices they have blamed the men of the moment for what the centuries had prepared."[50]

Meanwhile, if one asks what this intelligent woman and, with her, many authors even today mean by "what the centuries had prepared," it turns out that they mean the preparation, not of Jacobinism, but of a most salutary enterprise: the reform of

---

[49] Madame de Stael, *Considérations*, I, 47f.

[50] *Ibid.*, I, 1.

antiquated and degenerated institutions according to the demands of common sense and for the well-being of the nations. Overlooking the nature of the false theories, they assert that until 1789 there was a steady drift towards a desirable goal; that there were no deplorable deviations until later, through misunderstanding. In this manner these authors, perhaps without realizing or intending it, are led to distort history. The result is that they misjudge the true *course*, or the actual *character*, or the relative *importance* of the events. With a few examples of such distortions I should like to conclude this lecture.

An example of misjudging the real *course* of events is the complaint that Louis XVI stubbornly resisted the wishes and needs of the population, or, at the least, yielded to them with too little readiness.

It is not possible to be a pioneer of the Revolution with more obliging sympathy and zeal than were displayed by this youthful king. Half his reign was a steady anticipating of the wishes of the revolutionaries.[51] Mignet writes, "He succumbed because of his reform efforts. ... Up until the meeting of the Estates General his reign was nothing other than one long enterprise of ameliorations."[52] If you want a more extensive exposition, you will find

---

[51] † "It would require a volume by itself if one should wish to describe in detail the reform efforts from Louis' accession till the outbreak of the revolution." Sybel, *Geschichte*, I, 33. – Cf. Tocqueville, *L'Ancien Régime*, p. 288.

[52] Mignet, *Histoire*, I, 16.

it in the first volume of the anonymous German work that I recommended earlier;[53] but a cursory view is already sufficient. Who were his counsellors? I do not presume to weigh the talents and merits of Malesherbes, Turgot and Necker. I say only this: these men were revolution-minded with all their heart. Malesherbes was a passionate advocate of the new philosophy. Turgot acknowledged no right of corporation the moment it appeared to him to be injurious to the common good; for the common good was the highest law, and any respect for such a right was superstition.[54] In the same vein Necker wrote that the common good—that is, what is good for the majority—ought to be the guide for public administration.[55] Meanwhile, both these advisers of the Court, with freedom-loving intent, recommended the rankest arbitrariness: Necker considered liberty to be salutary only insofar as it is compatible with the common welfare,[56] and Turgot asserted that measures for the good of the nation must be executed even in opposition to the opinion of the representatives of its

---

[53] *Geschichte der Staatsveränderung in Frankreich unter König Ludwig XVI* (5 vols.; Leipzig, 1827-30).

[54] *Ibid.*, I, 162 [where reference is made to Turgot's article 'Fondation' in the *Encyclopédie*, VII (1st ed.; Paris, 1757), pp. 72, 75]. – † "In a way, Turgot prefigured the revolution." Jules Simon, *De la liberté politique*, p. 122.

[55] *Geschichte der Staatsveränderung*, I, 179 [where reference is made to Necker, *Sur la législation et le commerce des grains* (2nd ed.; Paris, 1775), I, 12; II, 155, 170].

[56] *Ibid.*, I, 183 [cf. Necker, *ibid.*, I, 174-177, 181-183].

free choice.[57] I cannot here insert the long chain of royal edicts by which the realization of these theories was attempted. The edicts are notable especially for their destruction of countless regulations which had been inherent in the proprietary rights of the towns and territories for centuries;[58] for their obliteration of provincial distinctions in the interest of revolutionary indivisibility.[59] Their common feature is to make everything new, to organize everything *à la Rousseau,* and so to reform the monarchy as to lead, with retention of the institution of kingship, to a revolutionary republic.

And so, with his ministers leading the way, the calm and modest Louis XVI was persuaded to actions similar to those of the turbulent and conceited Joseph II. He became the ally of the revolutionaries, and energetically so. Only when he experienced the injuriousness of reformatory violence did the grievous admission escape him: "Despotism is not good for anything, not even for forcing a people to be happy."[60]

That, in the second place, the *character* of the events has been misjudged is evident from the same illustration.

As the harvest of his zeal Louis soon reaped

---

[57] *Ibid.,* I, 233.

[58] See above, p. 00.

[59] [The first edition reads: ". . .centuries; for their splitting up of the realm in such a way as seemed to make possible the self-government of the people."]

[60] *Correspondance de Louis XVI,* I, 58.

repugnance and resistance. And now that he, unlike Joseph II, did not proceed further on the road of arbitrariness, in what light do you suppose his laudable "second thoughts" are made to appear? He did not have the vitality, writes Mignet, "to subject the privileged classes to the reforms."[61] His lack of resilience is then enlarged upon as though the issue were the disciplining of a despicable bunch of oppressors of the people. Forgotten is the fact that the so-called resistance of the privileged classes was but the dissatisfaction of men whose rights were being injured; that, moreover, in the language of the revolutionaries everything is labelled privilege which does not fit into the system of the new-fashioned equality; and, finally, that violation of the privileges directly or indirectly struck at the entire people.[62]

Allow me yet another illustration, the more so as it is important for judging subsequent events. I mean the interpretation of the widespread discussion in the months prior to the meeting of the National Assembly. Up to that time, it is said, the attitude of

---

[61] Mignet, *Histoire,* I, 16.

[62] Schlosser, though not an anti-revolutionary, writes: "The people clung to the old, and despotic rulers and ministers pulled it down. The sense of justice and tradition which is by nature characteristic of the people (but which, alas, must be offended in every revolution if anything of lasting benefit is to be accomplished) [I leave the author wholly responsible for this parenthetic clause – Gr. v. Pr.] recalcitrated as much against doctrinal as against physical violence. Hence the resistence against Pombal, Joseph II, Struensee, Gustavus III. Not just the privileged classes fought against these ministers and monarchs, but the people." *Geschichte*, III, 3.

those who longingly looked forward to change was irreproachable. It was "the sublime movement of 1789." Men talked of reform, not of revolution. "The revolution of 1789," we are told, "had as its only goal to regularize the limits of authority which have always existed in France."[63] And are you wondering what this statement is based on? It is based on the *cahiers de doléances*, the instructions drawn up for the deputies to the Estates General by the electoral colleges of the Nobility, the Clergy and the Third Estate. These *cahiers*, it is averred, bear witness everywhere to a genuinely monarchical spirit. I have here an excellent brochure entitled *Appel à la France contre la division des opinions,* a masterly survey of the revolution placed in instalments in the *Gazette de France* in 1831; in it I read an exuberant eulogy of the unanimity of 1789 for maintaining vested rights and the historic form of government:

When one takes a look into the *cahiers* of these meetings which were held simultaneously throughout the kingdom, one is stirred with admiration for the profound wisdom and the sense of order and equity that presided at their deliberations. Unity of desires, an almost miraculous harmony in the indication of the same abuses and the same reforms, unanimity in sentiment and behaviour: that is what is found in every one of the reports of these local assemblies. Everywhere the same love and the same gratitude toward the common father of the French; the same respect for acquired rights and for the fundamental principles of society. One can scarcely comprehend how such accord in desires and expressions could have

---

[63] Madame de Stael, *Considérations*, I, 145.

arisen in assemblies so diverse and among populations so widely separated. All social classes there agreed on what would be best for the fatherland. All interests melted together into the common interest. On the one side complete self-denial, on the other respect and cordiality, and on both sides a confident expectation of virtue and equity from the King. This is what can be read in every line of these monuments to the wisdom and goodwill of the people. Nothing is found in these *cahiers* that is not French and not national, that is not inspired by the truest and purest patriotism, that could not have realized a great perfecting of society for France and have opened for her an era of liberty, peace and happiness.[64]

Yet when we do take a closer look at the *cahiers,* of what nature is the highly praised spirit of the electors? They want the monarchy, yes, but which monarchy? The historical one or the revolutionary one? A monarchy in which the king is the sovereign of his subjects, or one in which he is the servant of the sovereign people? Look and see what is unanimously stated in the *cahiers* of the Nobility: the King is the *first official* and possesses the power that is *delegated* to him.[65]

Would you like more such samples from the *cahiers* of their so-called attachment to the historical constitutional law? The Nation is to be consulted about all that is of importance to it. All general laws must be made and sanctioned by the Estates. The legislative power belongs to the Nation, the executive

---

[64] *Appel à la France contre la division des opinions*, p. 7.
[65] Cf. above, p. 000.

power to the Monarch. The Third Estate demands double representation and voting by head.[66] The following judgment,[67] for all its terseness, is not too severe: "The *cahiers* were a twofold declaration of war: by the three estates on the monarch, and by the Third Estate on Nobility and Clergy."[68]

------

[66] †How incorrect is the assertion, "Of the ideas of Rousseau no trace is to be found in the *cahiers*: they do not begin to function until the revolution is well under way"! [The author here anonymously rebuked is Robert Fruin (1823-99). Later a historian of repute, Fruin made his debut in the scholarly world by attacking Groen in a study at once incisive and arrogant: *Het antirevolutionaire staatsregt van Mr. Groen van Prinsterer ontvouwd en beoordeeld* (Amsterdam, 1853); the sentence quoted by Groen is found on p. 17, or in *Verspreide Geschriften*, X, 90.] – Tocqueville writes: "These *cahiers*, the original manuscripts of which form a long series of volumes, will remain the testament of the old French society, the final expression of its wishes, the authentic announcement of its last will." *L'Ancien Régime,* p. viii. – The last will, yes, but it seems to me at the same time *the programme of the new society*, the programme which was to produce the opposite of what the nation then still wanted. Tocqueville himself,after all, also writes: "When I made a list of all these proposals I noticed with something like consternation that what was actually being asked for was the simultaneous and systematic abolition of all laws and all customs then current in the country. I saw at once that it was going to be a case of one of the vastest and most dangerous revolutions the world had ever seen." *Ibid.*, p. 219f.

[67] [The first edition reads: "Putting aside the question whether in many respects historical institutions were not, in good faith, mistakenly identified with the theoretical concepts, in any case the following judgment. . ."]

[68] "If the demands of the three estates were met, the King would find himself robbed simultaneously of all the real privileges of the supreme power and of all the necessary means to maintain it. From the master he would become the subject of his people. If the Third Estate could carry through the wishes in its *cahiers* with respect to the first two estates, their fate would be entirely in its hands: and its utterances

With the main issue thus neglected, many authors go wrong, thirdly, by exaggerating the importance of *secondary* matters.

This time I have a number of examples that are taken from a single page of Ancillon.[69] This talented author writes as follows:

Far from having to view the revolution as inevitable, one can adduce a host of facts which by their presence or absence would have prevented it or given it a different course. To these belong: (a) the invitation which in a certain sense was extended to all Frenchmen to discuss the manner of their representation; (b) the long interval between the convocation and the actual convening of the Estates General; (c) the doubling of the Third Estate; (d) the fixing of the meeting-place at Versailles, close to the Parisian volcano, instead of in Blois, Tours, Compiègne, or a similar town; (e) the timidity of the Court, which prevented it from settling the larger questions before the deputies had had time to come to an understanding with each other and reach agreement. If the declaration of June 20 had been made on May 5 it would have altered the entire situation in France.[70]

---

left them little hope for leniency. In essence the *cahiers* were a twofold declaration of war: by the three estates on the monarch, and by the Third Estate on Nobility and Clergy." *Geschichte der Staatsverän-derung*, II, 263.

[69] [The second edition adds: "a publicist and statesman who used to enjoy a well-deserved reputation and whose widely read publications contain many a remark worth laying to heart"; to which the footnote is appended: "Mr. Ancillon, publicist, historian, moralist and philosopher, without much originality or power in these diverse areas but everywhere judicious, clear-headed, and conciliatory." Guizot, *Mémoires*, IV, 19.]

[70] Ancillon, *Nouveaux Essais*, I, 98. – † Similar views are also

Now Ancillon certainly belongs to those authors who have a right, when one disagrees with them, to have their views tested, both as to basic premise and as to the facts adduced.

The basic premise is clear. Ancillon will not allow that the revolution was inevitable, at least not prior to June 1789:

To say that the revolution was inevitable is to say that the weakness of the Government and the criminal impertinence of the Assembly were necessary and inevitable. Let anyone who so desires adopt this view: it is as contrary to man's freedom as it is to his dignity, and it humiliates him by absolving him of responsibility for everything he does and everything he tolerates.[71]

This passage does not alarm me. Ancillon rejects the view that the revolution was inevitable on the grounds that it would cancel man's responsibility. I persist in my view that, in June 1789 as well as earlier, the French revolution was inevitable; but I protest against the inference. This view has nothing in common with fatalism,[72] with absolving crime or criminals. Or has it not been written, "It must needs be that offences come; but woe to that man by whom

---

presented by him in a very significant survey, "Ansicht der französischen Revolution," at the end of his book *Ueber Souveränität und Staats-Verfassungen,* pp. 76-102.

[71] Ancillon, *Nouveaux Essais,* I, 96.

[72] Cf. above, p. 000.

the offence cometh!"[73] The fact that a seductive error, once it has corrupted the human heart, will then manifest itself on that all too fertile soil in a bounteous harvest of misconceptions and misdeeds, does not mean that a man's guilt and accountability are annulled. And as for what I tolerate: the fact that I cannot prevent the evil that issues from men whose principles I condemn never obliges me to assist or applaud them.

Not impressed, however, by the irresistibility of principles once set in motion, Ancillon looks for an explanation solely in the deeds of those who, nominally at least, were "in power." Meanwhile he overlooks the temper of the atmosphere in which king and counsellors were caught up. In normal times it is altogether true: hesitation encourages rebellion and partial concessions made from weakness are the surest means to seeing oneself humiliated and constrained to give in completely. But these were not normal times. Those of whom such firmness is demanded—how could they, equally children of their age, have possessed it? And even if they had possessed such firmness by way of an exception which it would be hardly possible to explain, how could they ever have had the opportunity to assert their will in opposition to the will of practically everyone!

No one should be expected to keep his gait steady when universal intoxication is in the air. And

---

[73] Matt. 18:7.

even if one individual should somehow contrive to resist the fever of opinion, one should not fancy that, amid the passionate shouting and mad rushing by all, precisely that one individual, because he remains (to everyone else's indignation) sedate and sober, will be able to stay in control and carry the day. Madame de Stael's remark concerning the powerlessness of men like Lafayette is very true: "Whatever his political conviction might have been, his power would have been broken had he wanted to oppose the spirit of the time. In that epoch ideas ruled, not individuals. The tremendous will of Bonaparte himself would not have availed against the general direction of men's minds."[74] Is it conceivable, then, that a generation which had absorbed the ideas of Montesquieu and Rousseau as political gospel would have allowed itself to be prevented by some act or decision, wise deliberation or prudent manoeuvre on the part of the Court from marching in the sweep of the revolutionary theory?[75] It is from this viewpoint that we ought to consider the facts adduced by Ancillon.

The Estates General, he suggests, should have been convoked *as in 1614*. A splendid piece of

---

[74] Madame de Stael, *Considérations*, I, 378.

[75] † Ancillon deplores "the criminal impertinence of the Assembly" and "the weakness of the government," in particular with respect to the fact that the Estates General had constituted themselves as the National Assembly (*Nouveaux Essais*, I, 96). But here too, he forgets the keynote of everything that was taking place. From the standpoint of the prevailing doctrine, would a different attitude on the part of the Assembly not have been taken as miserable weakness, resistance by the King as "criminal impertinence"?

advice—but unfeasible. On that former basis the king was autocrat. The subjects were merely heard. Consent was asked only for subsidies. Does one seriously think that public opinion, aware of its superior strength, could have been appeased by such a mockery of its demands?

At least care should have been taken, we are told, not to double the number of deputies from the Third Estate, which automatically entailed voting by head and therefore victory for the democratic principle. To be sure, to prevent the revolution nothing would have been more desirable than to have had each estate deliberate separately, or to have seen to it, at least, that in their joint sessions the Third Estate could always be overruled by Nobility and Clergy. Such shrewd calculation, however, had but one shortcoming: the calculation that one is less than two was too obvious, too simple; the Third Estate, too, knew its arithmetic. Now that Clergy and Nobility were both objects of contempt; now that everybody knew, according to what was presumed to be common-sense politics, that the number of representatives should be proportional to the number of those represented—would now the Third Estate, which possessed the irresistible power in both number and theory, passively have acquiesced in being constantly overruled by the votes of a small and hated minority, a minority of hardly any account when compared with the total count of the population? Madame de Stael doubts it. Writes she: "If it had not been granted double representation legally, few doubted but that the Third Estate, irritated by not having obtained what it desired, would have sent a still greater number of deputies to the Estates General. . . . This was the mode. It was the upshot of the entire eighteenth century."[76] On this score, too, then, tradition was held to be in conflict with right and reason. It was in conflict with the very basis of natural law: strictly proportional representation. As Thiers puts it: "On the one hand hoary traditions were being adhered to, on the other hand natural rights and reason."[77]

Turning now to the timidity of the Court—from other authors we hear of a preventive exactly opposite to the one suggested by Ancillon: Madame de Stael and Thiers tell us that France could have been saved, not by inflexibility, but by more generous indulgence. The former says:

The Estates General were ushered in under the most auspicious portents . . . . Undoubtedly there still remained important points of discord between the nation and the privileged classes, but the position of the King was now such that he could be their arbiter by voluntarily reducing his power to that of a wisely limited monachy.[78]

So, a "wisely limited monarchy" would have warded off revolution! But what, pray tell, is the meaning of

---

[76] Madame de Stael, *Considérations,* I, 170, 172.

[77] Thiers, *Histoire,* I, 22.

[78] Madame de Stael, *Considérations*, I, 179f.

this term? The qualifier "wisely" is open to a variety of interpretations. In any event, let me remind you that the aspiration of the philosophy of that day was no longer to limit the power of the monarch but rather to secure the unlimited power of the sovereign people.

Thiers deems the actual concessions fruitless because they were too little and too late.

After the Nation had been promised a meeting of the Estates General, it demanded that the time of convocation be set earlier. This done, it wanted to dominate the assembly. This was refused, but the means to preponderance were placed in its hands through the doubling of its representation. Thus concessions were never made save in part, and only when resistance was no longer possible. But by this time the Nation's strength had grown and become palpable, and it wanted to have everything it thought it could get. The continual resistance which stimulated its ambition was soon to make that ambition insatiable. But even then, if a great minister, infusing a little strength into the King, winning the Queen over to his side, and restraining the privileged classes, had in one stroke surpassed and satiated the desires of the Nation by granting a liberal constitution himself; if he had satisfied the Nation's sense of the need for action by immediately summoning it, not to reform the state's constitution but to discuss its annual interests in a state already constituted—if this had been done, the struggle might never have begun.[79]

Granted, when there is cause for grievance one should

---

[79] Thiers, *Histoire*, I, 25.

of his own accord and without delay comply with demands that are fair, so as to be able to be all the firmer against unfair demands. And indeed, if passions are appeased by timely and generous grants, they are incited by extorted semi-concessions. I have no objection against this traditional wisdom, save that I do not consider it applicable in this case. For in 1789 the Court was confronted by a doctrine according to which everything that the people demanded seemed but their indisputable right, all that they obtained but an advance payment, a partial redemption of an unpayable debt. Satiation is inconceivable in the case of the Revolution spirit because it has the power to devour everything. Abundance of water is insufficient for a bottomless vessel.

It seems to me that Madame de Stael is perfectly correct when she observes:

Examining the conduct of Louis XVI one can certainly find mistakes in it, albeit that some reproach him with not having defended his unlimited power deftly enough whereas others accuse him of not having yielded sincerely to the enlightened insights of the age. But his mistakes were so in the nature of the circumstances that they reappeared almost as often as the same combinations of circumstances repeated themselves.[80]

From this last observation, however, one must not borrow yet another excuse: namely, that the

---

[80] Madame de Stael, *Considérations*, I, 48.

mistakes of Louis must be charged to the circumstances: under different circumstances the outcome would have been better. No, the circumstances could not have been more favourable. Or rather, in the atmosphere of that time all circumstances turned unfavourable. No matter what the King might have done or left undone, once the Revolution had conquered the minds it was bound to subject every circumstance to itself and be reinforced by resistance and indulgence alike.

This conquest of the minds was unmistakable, and history would now bring to light what had already been concluded in the sphere of thought. It is from this perspective that the events are to be appraised as to their origin, nature and importance. Examples are numerous.

Take the famous pamphlet by Sieyes on *The Third Estate*. With such questions and answers as: "What has it been? Nothing. What is it? Everything. What does it ask to be? Something!"[81] it had incalculable influence. But why? Because it was the succinct summary of the long applauded reasoning concerning the supremacy of the people.

Take the union of the estates into the National Assembly. Madame de Stael's characterization is indeed not too strong: "This decree was the revolution itself."[82] Yet this promulgation of the

---

[81] Sieyes, *Qu'est-ce que le tiers état?* [(Paris, Jan. 1789), opening sentences].

[82] Madame de Stael, *Considérations*, I, 204.

revolution, this vanishing of the privileged estates into a body representing the people as a whole was but the first step in applying a theory which had already triumphed.

Take the mutually competitive assaults on the privileges during the infamous night of August 4, 1789. The results were sweeping, and yet this general destruction was the execution of a verdict pronounced long ago.[83]

But to continue like this would carry us into the phase of Development, for which I have reserved the next lecture. I have said enough if I have shown how in 1789 the Preparation, now that it was complete, had to be followed by the Development. Even Ancillon, somewhat inconsistently, admits:

As to its principles the revolution was consummated the day the Third Estate proclaimed itself the National Assembly; as to its means the revolution was consummated the day the people captured the Bastille. On the first day the sovereignty of the

---

[83] †Repeatedly it is said: Had this or that happened or not happened, the revolution would have been checked. There is no end of examples. – Had Louis XVI but listened in 1775 to Turgot, who sought a merely advisory body of representatives of the people! *Answer:* "The scope of such a measure and the spirit of the age could not have been more misjudged. True, towards the close of revolutions it has often been possible to do with impunity what Turgot proposed: grant the shadow of liberty without its substance. . . . But in the early stages of a revolution such methods always fail; they achieve nothing but to whet the people's appetite without satisfying it." Tocqueville, *L'Ancien Régime*, p. 221. See also above, p. 000. – Had the Duke of Brunswick

people was decreed. On the second the power of the mob was employed. Now the entire revolution is nothing but the development of this principle and of this means, which had to lead to the sovereignty of the mob.[84]

Ancillon dates the inevitability of the French revolution from the decree by which the National Assembly constituted itself[85] —forgetting that this very act was itself inevitable: the theory of the supremacy of the people, master of the minds owing to the spirit of the age, was not to be stopped in its pursuit of a corresponding state. The eruption of a volcano is inevitable long before the mountain-mass is torn asunder. The French revolution was inevitable long before it broke out.

What we witness in 1789 is the Revolution. It is not "a political reformation which in spite of its attendant evils belongs in goal and outcome to the salutary events of world history," as some authors claim. It is more than just a political revolution

---

not proclaimed his Manifesto in 1792, the throne would not have fallen! *Answer*: "According to the testimony of contemporaries the Manifesto made practically no impression at all on the French people. It was a setback of the greatest significance precisely because it remained so completely without effect." Sybel, *Geschichte*, I, 501.

[84] Ancillon, *Nouveaux Essais*, I, 97.

[85] † *From that time on* the unleashed revolution, also according to Ancillon, had to have free course. "From the moment the King recognized the National Assembly, everything that followed happened as a matter of course and *had to happen that way*. . . . The revolution was not corrupted through coincidences, but was from the beginning a terrible corruption of man's inherent striving after perfection, a mad exaggeration of all emotions and ideas, and the result, especially, of an

ending in democracy, as one would gather from Ancillon's formulation. It is the Revolution: with its baleful influence which, though tempered in its pernicious effect by the blessings of a higher providence, continues even in our day to frustrate the operation of truly wholesome principles. It is the Revolution: with its systematic application of the philosophy of unbelief; with its atrocities and destructiveness; with its self-deification and its adoration of Reason on the ruins of the ancient state.

In view of the predominance of the false philosophy this could have been predicted. And it was predicted. For instance, as early as 1770 the king was told by the clergy: "Impiety bears a grudge against both God and men. It will not be satisfied until it has destroyed all authority, divine and human. It will plunge France into all the horrors of anarchy and give birth to the most unspeakable revolutions."[86]

Lacretelle relates a curious event that took place

---

enormous misconception, of a great and chronic basic error. For, the moment the National Assembly rose omnipotent from the ashes of the Estates General, there came along with it and in it as the supposed principle of life the principle of political death, and as the foundation of the work to be commenced the very mine which was inevitably to blow it to pieces: POPULAR SOVEREIGNTY *reared its mighty head* – that all-shattering Giant who smashed as it was being raised the very structure he was intended to sustain and who kept in ceaseless turmoil what was supposed to repose upon him." Ancillon, *Ueber Souveränität*, pp. 81f.

[86] Soulavie, *Mémoires*, I, 219, 222. [In their General Assembly of 1770 the clergy of France petitioned the King to suppress books like Holbach's *Système de la Nature.*]

during Lent 1789. In a sermon for the Court at Paris, in the Cathedral of Notre Dame, Father Beauregard delivered the following prophetic words[87] in a thundering voice:

Yea, Lord, Thy temples will be plundered and destroyed, Thy festivals abolished, Thy name blasphemed, Thy worship proscribed. But what do I hear? Great God, what do I see? Thy sacred hymns of praise, which made Thy glory resound through the hallowed vaults—they are being exchanged for songs lewd and profane! And you, vile goddess of paganism—you are rudely entering here to take the place of the living God and occupy the throne of the Saint of saints, to receive the accursed incensing of your new worshippers! [88]

What happened in 1789 had to happen. And in contrast to Ancillon's overestimation of the act by which the particular title "National Assembly" was adopted, you will rather, I think, set your seal to the pithy statement of Mignet, an author to whom has fallen the gift of often sketching the essence of the most important events with a single stroke: "The Estates General announced a revolution that had already been made."[89]

---

[87] [Cf. below, p. 000.]

[88] Quoted in Ch. Lacretelle, *Histoire de France pendant le dix-huitième siècle.* VII, 11.

[89] Mignet, *Histoire,* I, 36. — †"When King Louis XVI convoked the estates of the realm, the revolution had already taken full possession of the national consciousness." Stahl, *Philosophie des Rechts,* III, 360. — "As soon as public opinion had obtained an organ for its power in the Estates General, it needed only to state its will, indeed only to state the facts of the situation, and the old, decrepit state irretrievably crumbled into pieces." Sybel, *Geschichte* I, 46.

BIBLIOGRAPHY
CHRONOLOGY

BIBLIOGRAPHY

Alison, A. *History of Europe from the Commencement of the French Revolution in 1789 to the Restoration of the Bourbons in 1815.* 10 vols. Paris, 1841-42.

Ancillon, Fr. *Nouveaux essais de politique et de philosophie.* 2 vols. Paris and Berlin, 1824.

———— *Ueber Souveränität und Staats-Verfassungen. Ein Versuch zur Berichtigung einiger politischen Grundbegriffe.* 2nd ed. Berlin, 1816.

Appel à la France contre la division des opinions. Extract from the *Gazette de France.* [By H. de Lourdoueix.] Paris, 1831.

Baird, R. *Religion in the United States of America. Or an Account of the Origin, Progress, Relations to the State and Present Condition of the Evangelical Churches in the United States. With Notices of the Unevangelical Denominations.* Glasgow and Edinburgh, 1844.

———— *De la religion aux Etats-Unis d'Amérique.* French trans. by L. Burnier. 2 vols. Paris, 1844.

Berliner politisches Wochenblatt. Berlin, 1831-1838.

Burke, E. *Works.* 8 vols. London, 1823.

Correspondance de Louis XVI. 2 vols. Paris, 1803. [Apocryphal.]

62

Croker, J. W. *Essays on the Early Period of the French Revolution.* London, 1857.

Fruin, R. *Het antirevolutionaire Staatsregt van Mr. Groen van Prinsterer ontvouwd en beoordeeld.* Amsterdam, 1853.

—— *Verspreide Geschriften.* Vol. X: *Redevoeringen en*
—— *Opstellen van verschillende aard II.* The Hague, 1905.

Geschichte der Staatsveränderung in Frankreich unter König Ludwig XVI. [By Carl Heinrich von Schütz.] 5 vols. Leipzig, 1827-30.

Groen van Prinsterer, G. (ed.) *Archives ou correspondance inédite de la Maison d'Orange-Nassau.* Première Série. 10 vols. Leyden, 1835-47.

—— *Grondwetherziening en Eensgezindheid.* Amsterdam, 1849.

—— *Handboek der Geschiedenis van het Vaderland.* Leyden, 1845.

—— *Ter Nagedachtenis van Stahl.* Amsterdam, 1862.

—— *Proeve over de Middelen waardoor de Waarheid wordt gekend en gestaafd.* 2nd ed. Amsterdam, 1858.

—— *Verscheidenheden over Staatsregt en Politiek.* Amsterdam, 1850.

—— *Verspreide Geschriften. Eerste Deel: Staatsregt en Politiek.* Amsterdam, 1859.

Guizot, F. P. G. *Mémoires pour servir à l'histoire de mon temps.* 8 vols. Paris and Leipzig, 1858-67.

—— *Pourquoi la révolution d'Angleterre a-t-elle réussi?*
—— *Discours sur l'histoire de la révolution d'Angleterre.* Paris and Brussels, 1850.

Haller, Ch. L. de. *Restauration de la science politique, ou théorie de l'état social naturel, opposée à la fiction d'un état civil factice.* Revised and translated, from the second German edition, by the author. 6 vols. Lyons and Paris, 1824-75. Vol. I: *Exposition, histoire*

63

et critique des faux systèmes de l'école. Principes généraux de l'ordre naturel ou divin, opposés à ces systèmes. Lyons and Paris, 1824.

Heeren, A. H. L. *Handbuch der Geschichte des europäischen Staatensystems und seiner Colonien, von der Entdeckung beyder Indien bis zur Errichtung des Französischen Kaiserthums.* 3rd ed. Göttingen, 1819.

Instruction of Her Imperial Majesty to the Commissioners for Composing a New Code of Laws. St. Petersburgh, 1767. English trans., 1768.

Journal des débats. Paris, 1789- .

Lacretelle, Ch. de. *Histoire de France pendant le XVIIIe siècle.* 14 vols. Paris, 1808-26.

Lamennais, F. de. *Oeuvres complètes.* Edited and revised by the author. 2 vols. Brussels, 1839.

Mallet du Pan, J. *Mémoires et correspondance pour servir à l'histoire de la révolution française.* Collected and edited by A. Sayous. 2 vols. Paris, 1851.

Mignet, F. A. A. *Etudes et portraits politiques.* Brussels, 1841.

_____ *Histoire de la révolution française, depuis 1789 jusqu'en 1814.* 5th ed. 2 vols. Paris, 1833.

Necker, J. *De la révolution française.* 2 vols. Paris, 1797.

Nederlandsche Gedachten. The Hague, 1829-32.

Quarterly Review. London, 1809- .

Renan, Ernest. "De l'influence spiritualiste de M. Victor Cousin; à propos de ses *Fragmens et souvenirs.*" In *Revue des deux mondes*, 28e Année (1858), Tome XIV, pp. 497-520.

Revue des deux mondes. Paris, 1831-1944.

Rousseau, J. J. *Oeuvres.* Nouvelle édition, revue, corrigée et augmentée. 11 vols. Amsterdam, 1769-72.

Schlosser, Fr. Chr. *Geschichte des achtzehnten Jahrhunderts und des neunzehnten bis zum Sturz des französischen*

Kaiserreichs. Mit besonderer Rücksicht auf geistige Bildung. 6 vols. Heidelberg, 1836-48.

Sieyes, E. J. *Qu'est-ce que le tiers état?* Paris, 1789.

Simon, J. *De la liberté politique.* 3rd ed. Paris, 1867.

Soulavie, J. L. *Mémoires historiques et politiques du règne de Louis XVI, depuis son mariage jusqu'à sa mort.* 6 vols. Paris, 1801.

Stael, Madame la baronne de. *Considérations sur les principaux événemens de la révolution françoise.* Published posthumously by M. le duc de Broglie and M. le baron de Stael. 3 vols. Paris, 1818.

Stahl, Fr. J. *Die gegenwärtige Parteien in Staat und Kirche.* Neunundzwanzig akademische Vorlesungen. Berlin, 1863.

―――― *Parlamentarische Reden.* Edited by J. P. M. Treuherz. Berlin, n.d. [1856].

―――― *Philosophie des Rechts.* 3rd ed. 3 vols. Heidelberg, 1854-56.

―――― *Die Revolution und die constitutionelle Monarchie.* Eine Reihe ineinandergreifender Abhandlungen. 2nd ed. Berlin, 1849.

Sybel, H. von. *Geschichte der Revolutionszeit von 1789 bis 1795.* 2nd ed. 3 vols. Düsseldorf, 1859-60.

Thiers, A. *Histoire de la révolution française.* Second edition, revised by the author. 10 vols. Liège, 1828-29.

Tocqueville, A. de. *L'Ancien Régime et la Révolution.* Paris, 1856.

―――― *Correspondance inédite d'Alexis de Tocqueville.* Published, with a Foreword, by Gustave de Beaumont. 2 vols. Paris, 1861.

―――― *Oeuvres complètes.* Edited by Madame de Tocqueville and Gustave de Beaumont. 9 vols. Paris, 1864-66.

Wachsmuth, W. *Geschichte Frankreichs im Revolutionszeitalter.* 4 vols. Hamburg, 1840-44.

CHRONOLOGY OF THE REVOLUTION

1750   Malesherbes becomes director of the *Librairie* and facilitates the appearance in France of publications by the *philosophes.*

1751   Publication of the first volume of the *Encyclopédie.* Voltaire, at the invitation of Frederick the Great, takes up residence in Prussia (till 1753).

1759   Pombal expels the Jesuit order from all Portuguese dominions.

1762   Publication of *Du contrat social* by Jean Jacques Rousseau.

1767   Catherine the Great of Russia issues her *Instruction* to a committee drafting a Code of laws. Aranda puts education under the control of the Spanish state.

1770   Publication of *La système de la Nature* by Baron d'Holbach.

1772   Gustavus III imposes a constitution upon Sweden along the lines of French enlightened thought.

1774 - 1792 Louis XVI king of France

1776 Turgot abolishes the urban guilds in France.

1779 Necker introduces provincial assemblies in France in which the third estate has double representation.

1780 - 1790 Joseph II Holy Roman emperor: prescribes the use of German in all schools throughout his lands, reorganizes the parishes, secularizes church lands, dissolves all monasteries of the contemplative orders, and places the seminaries for the clergy under state supervision.

1787 *Summer*: Revolutionary unrest in Holland: the Patriot societies and free corps are suppressed only after Prussian intervention.
Nov.: Louis XVI promises a meeting of the Estates General which has not convened since 1614.

1788 *July*: King Louis formally requests that information and recommendations be sent to him concerning the procedures to be observed in summoning the Estates General, in order to assure to the assembly constitutional correctness and popular confidence.
Aug.: The King announces his intention to convoke the Estates General to meet the next May.
Dec.: The King decrees that the number of deputies of the third estate shall be equal to that of the two upper estates combined.

1789 *Jan.*: Publication of a pamphlet by the abbé Sieyes entitled *Qu'est-ce que le tiers état?* , in which it is argued that the third estate constitutes a complete nation, hence that a meeting of its deputies constitutes a national assembly.

Jan. 24: Official convocation of the Estates General, accompanied by instructions for the election of deputies.

Feb. - April: Throughout the realm, local meetings of each of the three estates draw up their *cahiers de doléances.*

May 5: Opening session of the Estates General at Versailles.

June 10: The Third Estate invites the deputies of the other two estates to join them for common deliberation.

June 17: The Third Estate, in the presence of four thousand spectators, passes a motion adopting the title "National Assembly."

June 19: By a narrow margin the Clergy votes to join the Third Estate in a "General Assembly"; the dissident minority continues to meet separately.

June 20: The Tennis Court Oath: temporarily removed to an indoor tennis court, members of the "National Assembly" solemnly swear not to disband until the constitution of the realm is established and consolidated upon firm foundations.

June 23: The King orders the three estates to resume their separate meetings. The "National Assembly" refuses to comply.

June 24 - 26: More and more members of the Clergy, and also some of the Nobility, go over to the "National Assembly."

June 27: The King gives in and orders the remnants of Clergy and Nobility to meet with the other estates.

July 14: Paris crowds besiege the prison fortress *la Bastille,* effect the surrender of its garrison, and carry off its stores of gun-powder.

Aug. 4: In an evening session lasting till two in the morning, deputies of nobility and clergy surrender their feudal rights and tax immunities.

The Groen van Prinsterer Fund has been established to support the translation and publication of *Unbelief and Revolution* and other historic evangelical documents.

Your gift to the Fund would be especially useful and welcome at this time to help continue the work.

Please send your cheque or international money order to:

> THE GROEN VAN PRINSTERER FUND
> c/o Hoofdgebouw 13A−31
> Free University
> Amsterdam, the Netherlands

European remitters may use our bank-giro account no. 47.39.38.766 with the Amro Bank, Osdorpplein, Amsterdam (postal giro of bank: 1551000).